Make a
Joyful Sound

Make a Joyful Sound

Poems for Children by African-American Poets

Illustrated by
Cornelius Van Wright
and
Ying-Hwa Hu

Edited by Deborah Slier

Checkerboard Press ❖ New York

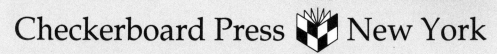

Poems selected by Deborah Slier Shine, Elizabeth Turner, and Denise Lewis Patrick.

———————————

Special thanks to the librarians and staff at the Schomberg Center for Research In Black Culture in New York, the librarians at the Central Children's Room in the Donnell Library Center of the New York Public Library, Ademola Olugebefola, and Abiodun Oyewole.

———————————

ACKNOWLEDGMENTS

Every effort has been made to trace the ownership of all copyrighted material and to secure the necessary permissions to reprint these selections. In the event of any question arising as to the use of any material, the editor and the publisher, while expressing regret for any inadvertent error, will be happy to make the necessary correction in future printings.

Thanks are due to the following for permission to reprint the copyrighted materials listed below:

GWENDOLYN BROOKS "Andre," "Rudolph is Tired of the City," "Timmy and Tawanda," and "Tommy" from *Bronzeville Boys and Girls* by Gwendolyn Brooks and illustrated by Ronni Solbert, copyright © 1956 by Gwendolyn Brooks Blakely. Reprinted by permission of HarperCollins Publishers. "To Don at Salaam" and "A Welcome Song for Laini Nzinga" from *To Disembark* © 1981 by Gwendolyn Brooks. Reprinted by permission of Third World Press, Chicago.

JOHN HENRIK CLARKE "The Poet Speaks" © 1948 by John Henrik Clarke. Reprinted by permission of the author.

LUCILLE CLIFTON "September" © 1974 by Lucille Clifton. Reprinted from *Everett Anderson's Year* by permission of Curtis Brown, Ltd.

COUNTEE CULLEN "Under the Mistletoe" is reprinted by permission of GRM Associates, Inc., agents for the estate of Countee Cullen. From the book *Copper Sun* by Countee Cullen © 1927 by Harper & Row; copyright renewed 1955 by Ida M. Cullen.

MARI EVANS "Who Can Be Born Black" from *Nightstar*, published by CAAS, University of California, at Los Angeles, 1981. Reprinted by permission of the author.

KARAMA FUFUKA "Big Mama," "My Daddy is a Cool Dude," "Parades," "Pretty Brown Baby," and "Summer Vacation" from *My Daddy is a Cool Dude and Other Poems* © 1975 by Karama Fufuka. Reprinted by permission of Dial Books For Young Readers.

NIKKI GIOVANNI "Knoxville, Tennessee" from *Black Feeling, Black Talk, Black Judgement* by Nikki Giovanni © 1968, 1970 by Nikki Giovanni. Reprinted by permission of William Morrow & Co., Inc. "Winter Poem" from *My House* by Nikki Giovanni © 1968 by Nikki Giovanni. Reprinted by permission of William Morrow & Co., Inc.

Table of Contents

Dedication

To all God's children–C V W & Y H

For Anna Ngutha, a Zulu mother–D S

Make a joyful sound : poems for children by African American poets /
illustrated by Cornelius VanWright and Ying-Hwa Hu.

    p. cm.

Includes index.

Summary: A collection of poems by Afro-American poets.

ISBN 1-56288-000-4 : $12.95

1. Children's poetry, American—Afro-American authors. 2. Afro-Americans—Juvenile poetry. [1. American poetry—Afro-American authors—Collections 2. Afro-Americans—Poetry.] I. VanWright, Cornelius, ill. II. Hu, Ying-Hwa, ill.

PS591.N4M32 1990

811.008'0896073—dc20

90-26284

CIP

AC

Besides all the marvelous things poetry is, it is also the practice of making concrete—putting into a communicable dimension—our thoughts and feelings. It is sharing our most profound and personal living spaces with people who then go from being strangers to being co-travelers on life's marvelous excursions into better understandings. It can lead to action. It can lead to love.

—*Ruby Dee*

NATIONHOOD

Nationhood
is black boys and girls
helping each other
to build a better world

BUILD NATION
NATION BUILD

The nation is each of us
No matter what we do
And every person has a job
To help make it come true

NATION BUILD
BUILD NATION

Nationhood
is black people everywhere
respecting each other
and doing their share

BUILD NATION
NATION BUILD

The nation is what we make it
No better or no worse
That's why it's so important
The nation always comes first

WE HAVE A NATION
WE HAVE A NATION

Useni Eugene Perkins

14

BY MYSELF

When I'm by myself
And I close my eyes
I'm a twin
I'm a dimple in a chin
I'm a room full of toys
I'm a squeaky noise
I'm a gospel song
I'm a gong
I'm a leaf turning red
I'm a loaf of brown bread
I'm a whatever I want to be
An anything I care to be
And when I open my eyes
What I care to be
Is me

Eloise Greenfield

15

TIMMY AND TAWANDA

It is a marvelous thing and all
When aunts and uncles come to call.
For when our kin arrive (all dressed,
On Sunday, in their Sunday-best)
We two are almost quite forgot!
We two are free to plan and plot.
Free to raid Mom's powder jar;
Free to tackle Dad's cigar
And scatter ashes near and far;
Free to plunder apple juice;
Let our leaping Rover loose.
Lots of lovely things we two
Plot and plan and quickly do
When aunts and uncles come to call,
And rest their wraps in the outer hall.

Gwendolyn Brooks

16

SEPTEMBER

I already know where Africa is
and I already know how to
count to ten and
I went to school every day last year,
why do I have to go again?

Lucille Clifton

KNOXVILLE, TENNESSEE

I always like summer
best
you can eat fresh corn
from daddy's garden
and okra
and greens
and cabbage
and lots of
barbecue
and buttermilk
and homemade ice-cream
at the church picnic
and listen to
gospel music
outside
at the church
homecoming
and go to the mountains with
your grandmother
and go barefooted
and be warm
all the time
not only when you go to bed
and sleep

Nikki Giovanni

NOPQRSTUVWXYZ

SUMMER VACATION

We read books in school
and we write stories
about what we did on
summer vacation.

This summer,
I played ball
and went to the beach
and Mama brought home
a brand-new baby.

Karama Fufuka

mommy daddy and baby

POEM

I loved my friend.
He went away from me.
There's nothing more to say.
The poem ends,
Soft as it began —
I loved my friend:

Langston Hughes

20

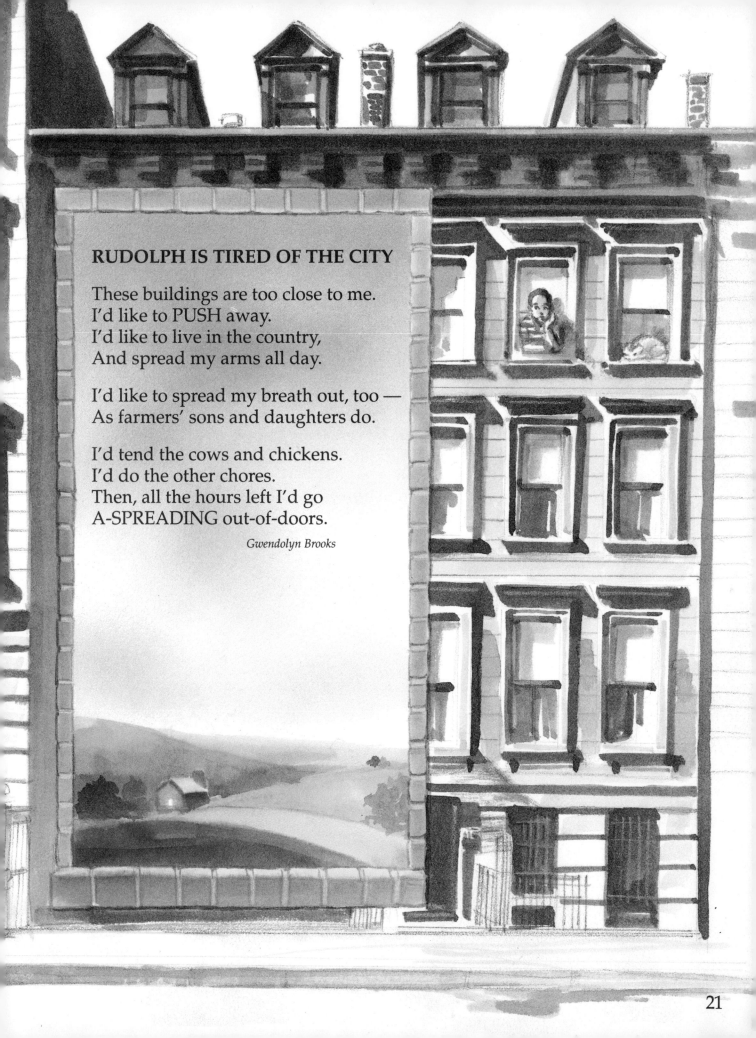

RUDOLPH IS TIRED OF THE CITY

These buildings are too close to me.
I'd like to PUSH away.
I'd like to live in the country,
And spread my arms all day.

I'd like to spread my breath out, too —
As farmers' sons and daughters do.

I'd tend the cows and chickens.
I'd do the other chores.
Then, all the hours left I'd go
A-SPREADING out-of-doors.

Gwendolyn Brooks

21

PARADES

I like to see parades
with the marching bands
and big bass drums;
They make me want to dance
and clap my hands.

Ladies ride in convertible cars
and smile and wave at you
and clowns come down the street
and make you laugh.

A parade makes everybody happy;
people talk and dance and sing—
I like to watch parades
more than any other thing.

Karama Fufuka

JOHN COLTRANE DITTY

John be playin'
I be swayin'
help me git dat jazz

He be tootin'
I be hootin'
help me git dat jazz

I be crowin'
while he blowin'
funky razamataz

John be screechin'
I be r e a c h i n'
reachin' out for jazz!

Dakari Kamau Hru

LITTLE SOUL SISTER

Little soul sister
In the dirty blue jeans
Prettiest little girl
That's on the scene

Want you to know
She's the sweetheart of the street
Ain't none like her
For she's hard to beat

Little soul sister
With the big smiling face
Even her skinny legs
Are a picture of grace

She's Queen Nefertiti
And Cleopatra too
There's nothing in the world
That is more true

Little soul sister
Little soul sister

She's got it all together

Useni Eugene Perkins

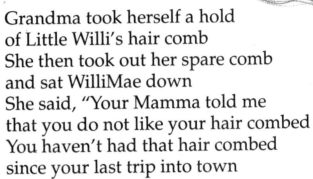

WILLIMAE'S CORNROWS

WilliMae, she wouldn't, wouldn't
wouldn't get her hair combed
She wouldn't get her hair combed
No matter how Ma tried
WilliMae would pout and stamp
and fuss over the hair comb
She didn't want her hair combed
My goodness how she'd cry

Grandma took herself a hold
of Little Willi's hair comb
She then took out her spare comb
and sat WilliMae down
She said, "Your Mamma told me
that you do not like your hair combed
You haven't had that hair combed
since your last trip into town

"If you will just sit still until
your Gra'am can get that hair combed
you let me get that hair combed and
I promise, yes it's true,
That by the time I'm finished
you won't have to get your hair combed
again for quite some time because
I'll make cornrows for you"

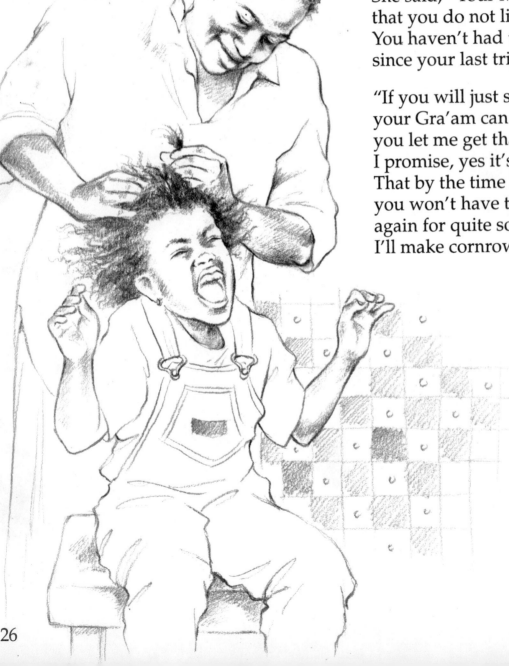

When Grandma first got started
WilliMae threw off a tantrum
She cried and cried so hard until
she finally fell asleep
She made herself so tired
with her fussing and her fighting
by the time Grandma was halfway through
you couldn't hear a peep

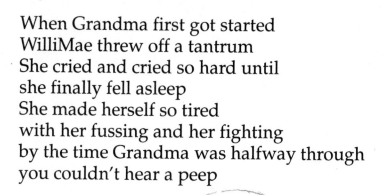

When WilliMae woke up again
it was an hour later
and Gra'am had finished braiding
pretty braids with beads of red
And Willi thought, 'How wonderful!'
when she looked in the mirror
and saw the pretty patterns
and red beads atop her head

She hugged and kissed her Grandma
and she promised her that next time
she wouldn't put up such a fuss
When it came time to comb
And that she'd be a little neater
even during playtime,
at nighttime and in daytime
'cause she loved those cornrows so!

Nanette Mellage

CROWN

Can't stop watching you!
Pardon while I stare
Watching you in African locks
Love you for your hair.

Gently bouncing near your brow
Cupping 'round your ear
The poetry atop your head
Keeps me coming near.

Swirling, sassy spiral-strands
Swing like swizzle sticks.
Laughing locks lay lavishly
Look like licorice.

Can't stop watching you!
Crown extraordinare.
Don't wear no hat. Don't change a
    thing—
My baby has GOOD hair!

Shake your head and let your locks
Hang all loose and free.
Shake them locks for no one else
You belong to me.

I could take you all around
Let the people stare.
I would be so proud to holler,
"See my baby's hair!"

Even if you tie it back
And make a pony tail,
A train come speedin' down the track
Would have to jump the rail!

Can't stop watching you!
Crown extraordinaire.
Don't wear no hat. Don't change a thing—
My baby has GOOD hair!

Dakari Kamau Hru

BLACK IS BEAUTIFUL

Black is beautiful and so am I
Black is beautiful
that ain't no lie

Black is mellow
real mellow

Black is cool
real cool

Black is sweet
real sweet

Black is strong
real strong

Black is good
real good

Black is

   mellow
   cool
   sweet
   strong
   good

and beautiful

That ain't no lie.

Useni Eugene Perkins

GIRLS CAN, TOO!

Tony said: "Boys are better!
  They can . . .

    whack a ball,
    ride a bike with one hand
    leap off a wall."

I just listened
  and when he was through,
I laughed and said:

    "Oh, yeah! Well, girls can, too!"

Then I leaped off the wall,
  and rode away
With *his* 200 baseball cards
  I won that day.

Lee Bennett Hopkins

31

MILEHIGH JEFF THE GIANT HARE

Children, children, please beware
of MileHigh Jeff the Giant Hare
See, MileHigh Jeff can eat a lot
Regardless if it's his or not
So hide your carrots and your peas
and tell the mice to hide their cheese
But if you see him, better shoo
MileHigh eats mice and children too!

Nanette Mellage

32

SORRY, SORRY MRS. LORRY

Sorry, sorry Mrs. Lorry
couldn't keep from being sorry
Broke a plate,
"So sorry, Kate!"
Tripped the cat,
"So sorry, Nat!"
Missed the bus,
"So sorry, Gus!
Guess I'm late.
I broke Kate's plate
And tripped Nat Cat
Imagine that!"
Sorry, sorry Mrs. Lorry

Nanette Mellage

33

APRIL RAIN SONG

Let the rain kiss you.
Let the rain beat upon your head with silver liquid drops.
Let the rain sing you a lullaby.

The rain makes still pools on the sidewalk.
The rain makes running pools in the gutter.
The rain plays a little sleep-song on our roof at night—

And I love the rain.

Langston Hughes

THINGS

Went to the corner
Walked in the store
Bought me some candy
Ain't got it no more
Ain't got it no more

Went to the beach
Played on the shore
Built me a sandhouse
Ain't got it no more
Ain't got it no more

Went to the kitchen
Lay down on the floor
Made me a poem
Still got it
Still got it

Eloise Greenfield

35

FOR PEACE SAKE

For peace sake
we need to do our best.
For peace sake
let's put the hate to rest.
For peace sake
it never is too late.
For peace sake
let's rid our lives of hate.

I believe that we can
build a bridge to understand,
we're all in this together.
It never ever is too late,
together let's rid our lives of hate.
Let's do it for peace sake.

For peace sake
we need to do our best.
For peace sake
let's put love to the test.

Love is really what we need;
together we can plant the seed.
For peace sake let's work in harmony.
For peace sake,
for love and happiness,
for peace sake
and for all the rest.

I believe that we can
build a bridge to understand,
we're all in this together.
It never ever is too late,
together let's rid our lives of hate.
Let's do it, let's do it
for peace sake.

For peace sake
we can make it right.
For peace sake
it can happen overnight.
It's time to take a break
from bigotry and hate —
we have an equal place
within the human race.
Love is really what we need,
together we can plant the seed.
for peace sake let's work in harmony.

For peace sake
examine how you feel.
For peace sake
how much of it is real?
For peace sake,
if you only knew
what hate can do to you.

I believe that we can
build a bridge to understand,
we're all in this together.
It never ever is too late,
together let's rid our lives of hate.
Let's do, let's do,
for peace sake.

Cedric McClester

37

RHAPSODY

I am glad daylong for the gift of song,
For time and change and sorrow;
For the sunset wings and world-end things
Which hang on the edge of tomorrow.
I am glad for my heart whose gates apart
Are the entrance-place of wonders,
Where dreams come in from the rush and din
Like sheep from the rains and thunders.

William Stanley Braithwaite

HOPE

Sometimes when I'm lonely,
Don't know why,
Keep thinkin' I won't be lonely
By and by.

Langston Hughes

MY PEOPLE

The night is beautiful,
So the faces of my people.

The stars are beautiful,
So the eyes of my people.

Beautiful, also, is the sun.
Beautiful, also, are the souls of my people.

Langston Hughes

WHAT COLOR IS BLACK?

black is the color of
my little brother's mind
the grey streaks
in my mother's hair
black is the color of
my yellow cousin's smile
the scars upon my
neighbor's wrinkled face.
the color of
the blood we lose
the color of our eyes
is black.
our love of self
of others
brothers sisters
people of a thousand
shades of black
all one.
black is the color of
the feeling that we share
the love we must express
the color of our strength
is black.

Barbara Mahone

AFRICA

Africa the Mother of all mothers
the world is her child
and she feeds him well
Africa bathes her body in the Nile
and comforts her soul in the pyramids
She is the First Woman
    and her black skin
    and her coarse haïr
    and bright eyes
    and full lips and hips
to make a God take a second look
enriched the Earth
nourished the spirit
colored the universe
Africa she is the flower and the tree
    the river and the sea
    the sun and the moon
from midnight to high noon

Often times she's dancing
with gold around her ankles
and diamonds on her feet
Gems from the Gods
overflow in her backyard
    and when her sons play the drums
      and her daughters start to sing
every ear and heart
is held captive
in the rhythm of Africa's love

Music flows from her mouth when she speaks
and all her children dance with her
Africa we breathe to the rhythm
of her heart beat
her blood flows through our veins
like the Sea
We become a storm
when we don't feel the safety
of our Mother's caress
When Africa is gone
she leaves us in the dark
of artificial light
trying to tear our faces apart
with our bare hands
too blind to see Africa
smiling inside our Soul
When Africa is gone
there is no music only noise
there is no love only hate
there is no truth only lies
there is no life only death
when she is gone the world becomes a misfit
and the universe a villain

Abiodun Oyewole

COLOR

Wear it
Like a banner
For the proud —
Not like a shroud.
Wear it
Like a song
Soaring high —
Not moan or cry.

Langston Hughes

HAIKU

i have looked into
    my father's eyes and seen an
    african sunset.

Sonia Sanchez

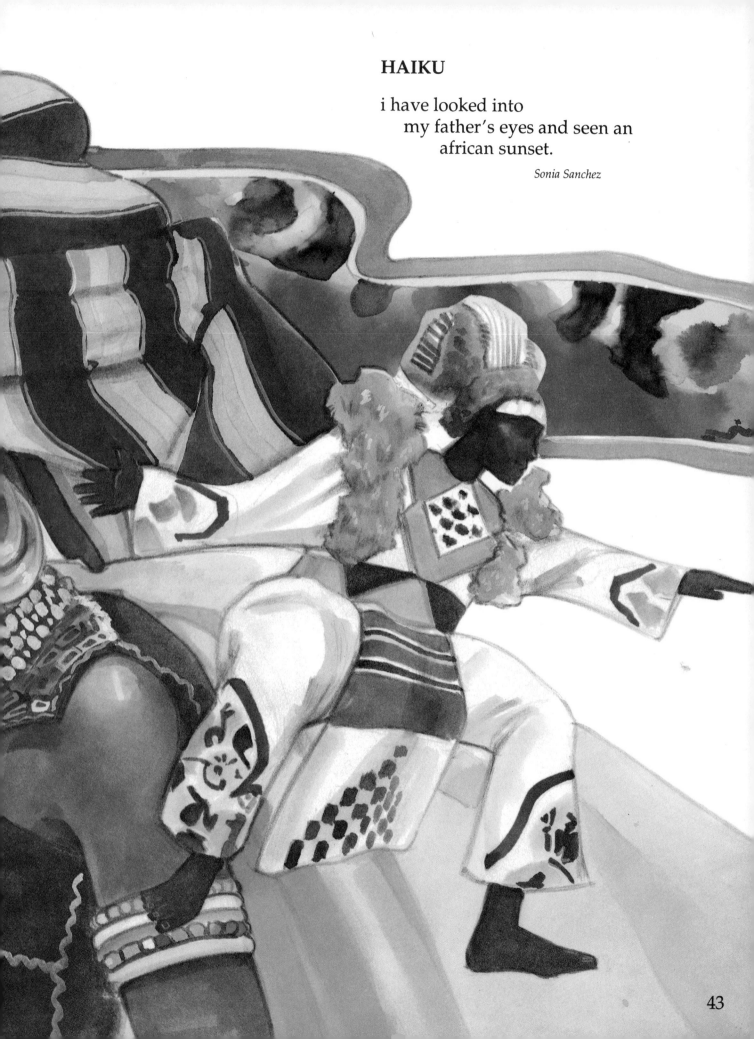

#4

Where my grandmother lived
there was always sweet potato pie
and thirds on green beans and
songs and words of how we'd
survived it all.
Blackness.
And the wind
a soft lull
in the pecan tree
whispered
Ethiopia
    Ethiopia, Ethiopia
E-th-io-piaaaaa!

Doughtry Long

PRETTY BROWN BABY

Pretty brown baby,
fat and fine;
love you, love you
all the time.

Karama Fufuka

44

AYO

her name
was Ayo

and as
she smiled

I saw teeth
white as ivory

but she was
more precious
than all the
ivory in Afrika

Useni Eugene Perkins

A WELCOME SONG FOR LAINI NZINGA
(Born November 24, 1975)

Hello Little Sister.
Coming through the rim of the world.
We are here! to meet you and to mold and
    to maintain you.
With excited eyes we see you.
With welcoming ears we hear the
clean sound of new language.
The language of Laini Nzinga.
We love and we receive you as our own.

Gwendolyn Brooks

THE MASK

I have a tribal mask
That brings up all my pride
I have a tribal mask
I feel so Black inside
Carved in fine mahogany
A face so dignified
I have a tribal mask
That brings up all my pride

Tribal markings on the forehead
And the nose and chin
High cheekbones in charcoal tones
Link me to my kin

When my mask is on my face
My ancestors call my name
When my mask is on my face
I know from whence I came
Though they're in the spirit world
They guide me just the same
When my mask is on my face
My ancestors call my name

Antique face with Bantu voice
Channeled through my space-age soul
Tribal elders speak through me
To get their story told

When I look out through the eyes
I see the Imbeleko* dance
When I look out through the eyes
I sense that it's my chance
To join in, leap and spin
And stomp into a trance
When I look out through the eyes
I see the Imbeleko dance

Dance for joy! A baby boy!
Beat that talking drum
The father names him Nkosi
And holds him to the sun

The spirit in the mask
Is my grandmother gone away
The spirit in the mask
Is here with me today
"Bring him here 'cause he's my
        chile!"
She always used to say
The spirit in the mask
Is my grandmother —
              here to stay!

Dakari Kamau Hru

*Xhosa word for celebration of childbirth.
Xhosa are a southern African people

AUNT SUE'S STORIES

Aunt Sue has a head full of stories.
Aunt Sue has a whole heart full of stories.
Summer nights on the front porch
Aunt Sue cuddles a brown-faced child to her bosom
And tells him stories.

Black slaves
Working in the hot sun,
And black slaves
Walking in the dewy night,
And black slaves
Singing sorrow songs on the banks of a mighty river
Mingle themselves softly
In the flow of old Aunt Sue's voice,
Mingle themselves softly
In the dark shadows that cross and recross
Aunt Sue's stories.

And the dark-faced child, listening,
Knows that Aunt Sue's stories are real stories.
He knows that Aunt Sue never got her stories
Out of any book at all,
But that they came
Right out of her own life.

The dark-faced child is quiet
Of a summer night
Listening to Aunt Sue's stories.

Langston Hughes

"KWANZAA IS . . ."

Kwanzaa is a holiday,
but unlike most,
does not convey
a religious observation
nor does it celebrate our nation.

And though our nation gave it birth,
it celebrates the cultural worth
of a darker continent
and the people that were sent.

People of a darker hue,
People much like me and you,
People whose great history
has been cloaked in mystery.

So Kwanzaa is
the time and place to reflect and retrace
the history missing from the books,
a time for taking second looks.

Kwanzaa is the poured libation
spilled in reverent observation
of the past that paved the way
for your people here today.

Kwanzaa is "nguzo saba,"
the seven principles that we harbor,
beginning with the unity
that makes us strong and helps us see
in perspective proper light
the other six that we recite.

One day after Christmas comes,
we listen to the Kwanzaa drums
and celebrate for seven days
our old customs and modern ways.

So Kwanzaa is our very own,
since 1966 it's grown
from a private observation
to one that's shared throughout the nation.

Cedric McClester

HARRIET TUBMAN

Harriet Tubman didn't take no stuff
Wasn't scared of nothing neither
Didn't come in this world to be no slave
And wasn't going to stay one either

"Farewell!" she sang to her friends one night
She was mighty sad to leave 'em
But she ran away that dark, hot night
Ran looking for her freedom

She ran to the woods and she ran through the woods
With the slave catchers right behind her
And she kept on going till she got to the North
Where those mean men couldn't find her

Nineteen times she went back South
To get three hundred others
She ran for her freedom nineteen times
To save Black sisters and brothers

Harriet Tubman didn't take no stuff
Wasn't scared of nothing neither
Didn't come in this world to be no slave
And didn't stay one either

And didn't stay one either

Eloise Greenfield

LULLABY
(For a Black Mother)

My little dark baby,
My little earth-thing,
My little love-one,
What shall I sing
For your lullaby?

Stars,
Stars,
A necklace of stars
Winding the night.

My little black baby,
My dark body's baby,
What shall I sing
For your lullaby?

Moon,
Moon,
Great diamond moon,
Kissing the night.

Oh, little dark baby,
Night black baby,

Stars, stars,
Moon,
Night stars,
Moon,

For your sleep-song lullaby!

Langston Hughes

WHO CAN BE BORN BLACK

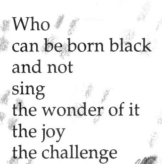

Who
can be born black
and not
sing
the wonder of it
the joy
the challenge

And/to come together
in a coming togetherness
vibrating with the fires of pure knowing
reeling with power
ringing with the sound above sound above sound
to explode/in the majesty of our oneness
our comingtogether
in a comingtogetherness

Who
can be born
black
and not exult

Mari Evans

55

A PROTEST POEM FOR ROSA PARKS

Every day for a long time now
I've been riding in the back
of the bus
sometimes I'm sitting
most times I'm standing
but if you look at my face
you can see my disgust
riding in the back of the bus
Now, today I'm real tired
just too tired to move
I done scrubbed floors
washed windows
I even polished ole Missy's shoes
the bus driver tells me
I got to give up my seat
'cause a white man wants it
and he just too good
to stand on his feet

Something in my gut
say I just don't give a damn
this seat I ain't givin' up
to hell with the white man
the white man he's waiting
for me to get up
and go to the back
I told him my feet hurt
and the back is already packed
You might as well
sound the alarm
and call the cops
this colored woman has gone mad
and she must be stopped
I didn't mind the handcuffs
or being in jail overnight
I still felt pretty strong
I guess I Knew I was right

Early that morning
revealed a brand-new day
A man named Martin Luther King
I was told was on his way
to see about me
and help Blacks get Equality
I felt good and started to sing
giving praise to the Lord
for Reverend Martin Luther King
when we first met
I'll never forget
the light in his eyes
and the Love on his face
he was our new Sunrise
to wake us up and win this Race
No matter how long
No matter how Blue
Martin was on a Mission
to make our dreams come true

We started the Montgomery Bus Boycott
and scared all the white folks in town
with Martin as our leader
we knew we would turn this thing around
we walked
used car pools
and worked together
with Victory in mind
having Faith that we'd win this battle
it was just a matter of time

The bus company went out of business
'cause WE didn't ride the bus
we discovered for the first time
the Power we had in US
Now when I look back
on that eventful day
I thank God and I pray
to never ever again
let anyone treat us like a slave

Abiodun Oyewole

BALLAD OF JOHN HENRY

John Henry was born
With a hammer in his hand
And no one in Alabama
Could really understand

    Hold your hammer, John Henry
    Hold your hammer, John Henry

At five years of age
He was strong as an ox
Could work all day
And never once stop

    Lift your hammer, John Henry
    Lift your hammer, John Henry

When he reached the age of ten
He could out hammer any man
And never went anyplace
Without his hammer in his hand

    Hit the steel, John Henry
    Hit the steel, John Henry

He yearned to work on the railroad
So he could hammer steel
Nothing else matter to him
Cause he had a strong will

    Hammer away, John Henry
    Hammer away, John Henry

And when he got the chance
To show what he could do
There wasn't a man around
That could hammer so hard and true

Don't give up, John Henry
Don't give up, John Henry

But one day he was challenged
To out hammer a machine
And though he did his best
He finally ran out of steam

The machine done won, John Henry
The machine done won, John Henry

And so John Henry died
Driving steel in the ground
But no one will deny
He was the best driver in town

You'll always be remembered, John Henry
You'll always be remembered, John Henry

Useni Eugene Perkins

MARTIN LUTHER KING JR.

Dr. King was a man
Who saw the mountain top
Who saw the mountain top
Dr. King was a man
Who saw the mountain top
And he did not stop

Glory Hallelujah
Glory Hallelujah

Dr. King was a man
Who climbed the mountain top
Who climbed the mountain top
Dr. King was a man
Who climbed the mountain top
Because he could not stop

Glory Hallelujah
Glory Hallelujah

Dr. King was a man
Who reached the mountain top
Who reached the mountain top
Dr. King was a man
Who reached the mountain top
Because he would not stop

Glory Hallelujah
Glory Hallelujah

Dr. King was a man
Who stood on the mountain top
Who stood on the mountain top
Dr. King was a man
Who stood on the mountain top
Because he would not stop

Free at last
Free at last

Useni Eugene Perkins

A POEM FOR "MAGIC"

(For Earvin "Magic" Johnson, Donnell Reid & Richard Franklin)

take it to the hoop, "magic" johnson
take the ball dazzling down the open lane
herk & jerk & raise your six feet nine inch
frame into air sweating screams of your neon name
"magic" johnson, nicknamed windex way back in high school
cause you wiped glass backboards so clean
where you first juked & shook
wiled your way to glory
a new style fusion of shake & bake energy
using everything possible, you created your own space
to fly through — any moment now, we expect your wings
to spread feathers for that spooky take-off of yours
then shake & glide, till you hammer home
a clotheslining deuce off glass
now, come back down with a reverse hoodoo gem
off the spin, & stick it in sweet, popping nets, clean
from twenty feet, right-side

put the ball on the floor, "magic"
slide the dribble behind your back, ease it deftly
between your bony, stork legs, head bobbing everwhichaway
up & down, you see everything on the court
off the high, yoyo patter, stop & go dribble, you shoot
a threading needle rope pass, sweet home to kareem
cutting through the lane, his skyhook pops cords
now lead the fast break, hit worthy on the fly
now, blindside a behind the back pinpointpass for two more
off the fake, looking the other way
you raise off balance into space
sweating chants of your name, turn, 180 degrees
off the move, your legs scissoring space, like a swimmer's
yoyoing motion, in deep water, stretching out now toward free flight
you double pump through human trees, hang in place
slip the ball into your left hand
then deal it like a las vegas card dealer
off squared glass, into nets, living up to your singular nickname
so "bad", you cartwheel the crowd toward frenzy
wearing now your electric smile, neon as your name

in victory we suddenly sense your glorious uplift
your urgent need to be champion
& so we cheer, rejoicing with you, for this quicksilver, quicksilver, quicksilver
moment of fame, so put the ball on the floor again, "magic"
juke & dazzle, shake & bake down the lane
take the sucker to the hoop, "magic" johnson, recreate reverse hoodoo
gems off the spin, deal alley-oop-dunk-a-thon-magician passes
now, double-pump, scissor, vamp through space
hang in place & put it all up in the sucker's face, "magic" johnson
& deal the roundball, like the juju man that you am
like the sho-nuff shaman man that you am
"magic," like the sho-nuff spaceman, you am

Quincy Troupe

PIGEONS AND PEANUTS FOR SALE

Arthur drove his truck from Georgia
up toward New York State
Went to sell pigeons and peanuts
at a special rate
> Drove through Petersburg, Virginia
> on his way up North
> Stopped for gas, he heard those pigeons
> flappin' back and forth

Figured he'd go back and see
what the fuss was about
But when he opened up the truck
the pigeons all flew out
> Them pigeons took the sack of nuts
> and tore it all to shreds
> All Arthur had was peanut shells
> and feathers on his head

Poor Arthur dusted himself off
and turned his truck around
With nothing left to sell up North
Arthur was Georgia bound
> When he got home he told his Dad
> about his rotten luck
> Dad scratched his head and then he said
> "Son, go reload that truck!"

Well, this time Arthur let the peanuts
ride up front with him
and left those pigeons in the back
to flap about at whim

When Arthur got to Petersburg
he didn't even stop
He didn't want this trip to turn
into another flop
He made it up to New York City
shortly before dark
Hung up his sign, put up his stand
right there in Central Park
When folks began to hear about
what Arthur had to sell
they came from parts both near and far
and business grew quite well
Soon Arthur realized that his
small venture was no lark
Folks buying peanuts and some pigeons
for their local parks
By now Old Arthur must have gone
through more than forty states
selling his pigeons and his peanuts
at a special rate
So if you see a bunch of pigeons
in a park or square
peckin' on peanuts in the grass
you know Old Art was there!

Nanette Mellage

65

BIG MAMA

Big Mama is my grandmother.
She lives down south.

When we go to visit her
we eat grits and sausage and
pork chops and eggs for breakfast,
and we get up real early.

Big Mama has a great big yard
and a swing on her porch.

Big Mama has a dog that catches
rabbits and at night
the stars are very bright.

Karama Fufuka

FINE BLACK KINFOLK

Fine Black kinfolk
Black as shade
Black as Cleopatra's braid

Black as smoke
Black as tar
Black as night in Zanzibar

Black as Tutankhamen's tomb
Black as an eclipse at noon

Fine Black beauties—
Black as pitch
Like oil wells
    Jet Black
    And rich!

Dakari Kamau Hru

BROTHERS

We're related — you and I,
You from the West Indies,
I from Kentucky.

Kinsmen — you and I,
You from Africa,
I from the U.S.A.

Brothers — you and I.

Langston Hughes

68

ANDRE

I had a dream last night. I dreamed
I had to pick a Mother out.
I had to choose a Father too.
At first, I wondered what to do,
There were so many there, it seemed,
Short and tall and thin and stout.

But just before I sprang awake,
I knew what parents I would take.

And *this* surprised and made me glad:
They were the ones I always had!

Gwendolyn Brooks

69

MY DADDY IS A COOL DUDE

When my daddy comes in from work
at night
he always say
"Hey man, gimme five"
and I lay it on him
and he smiles.

My daddy sure is a cool dude.

Karama Fufuka

LOVE DON'T MEAN

Love don't mean all that kissing
Like on television
Love means Daddy
Saying keep your mama company
    till I get back
And me doing it

Eloise Greenfield

TO DON AT SALAAM

I like to see you lean back in your chair
so far you have to fall but do not —
your arms back, your fine hands
in your print pockets.

Beautiful. Impudent.
Ready for life.
A tied storm.

I like to see you wearing your boy smile
whose tribute is for two of us or three.

Sometimes in life
things seem to be moving
and they are not
and they are not
there.
You are there.

Your voice is the listened-for music.
Your act is the consolidation.

I like to see you living in the world.

Gwendolyn Brooks

FATHER TO SON

Ain't you terible,
ain't you something,
getting up everyday
with a new dream
to come true.
Go on now and finish
building that pyramid
and then tell Daddy again
how a nation was conquered
because you cartwheeled
the Alps.
But don't use up all
your strength cutting up,
we still need you to show
us how to channel the
ocean's flow, so be careful
now and don't hurt yourself
showing off.

Alfred L. Woods

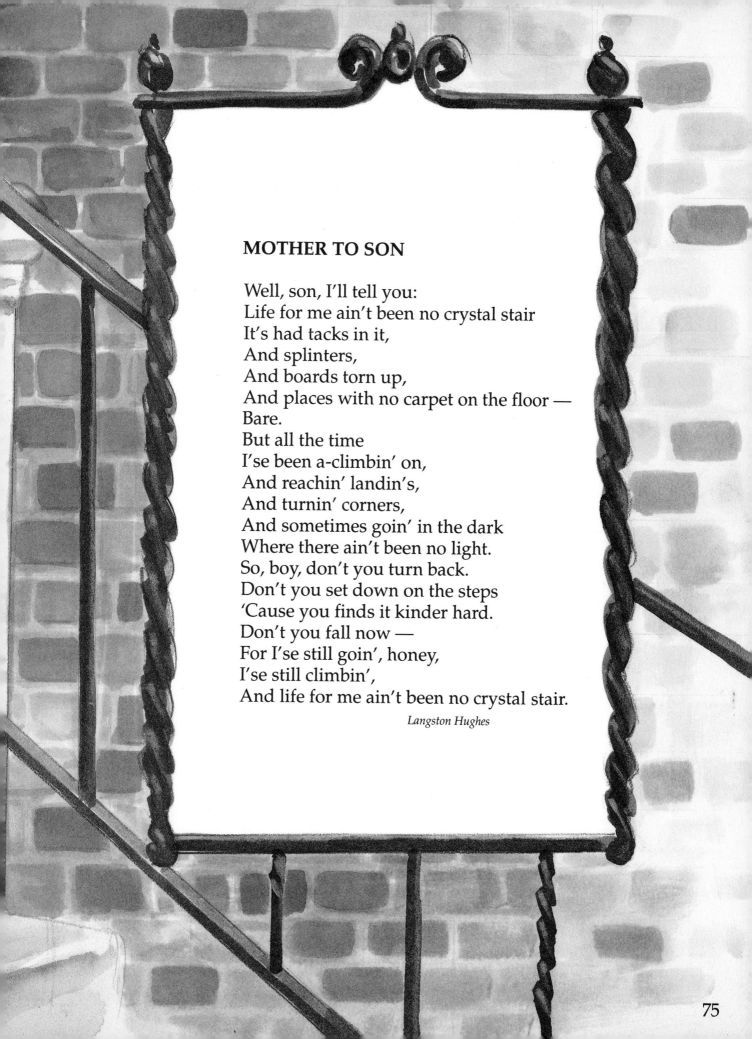

MOTHER TO SON

Well, son, I'll tell you:
Life for me ain't been no crystal stair
It's had tacks in it,
And splinters,
And boards torn up,
And places with no carpet on the floor —
Bare.
But all the time
I'se been a-climbin' on,
And reachin' landin's,
And turnin' corners,
And sometimes goin' in the dark
Where there ain't been no light.
So, boy, don't you turn back.
Don't you set down on the steps
'Cause you finds it kinder hard.
Don't you fall now —
For I'se still goin', honey,
I'se still climbin',
And life for me ain't been no crystal stair.

Langston Hughes

WHO AM I

love is my color
black is my color
beige is my color
red is my color
yellow is my color
love is my color

Kali Grosvenor

76

UNDER THE MISTLETOE

I did not know she'd take it so,
    Or else I'd never dared:
Although the bliss was worth the blow,
I did not know she'd take it so.
She stood beneath the mistletoe
So long I thought she cared;
I did not know she'd take it so,
Or else I'd never dared.

Countee Cullen

77

HEY BLACK CHILD

Hey Black Child
Do ya know who ya are
Who ya really are

Do ya know you can be
what ya wanna be
If ya try to be
What ya can be

Hey Black Child
Do ya know where ya goin
Where ya really goin

Do ya know ya can learn
What ya wanna learn
If ya try to learn
What ya can learn

Hey Black Child
Do ya know ya are strong
I mean really strong

Do ya know you can do
What ya wanna do
If ya try to do
What ya can do

Hey Black Child
Be what ya can be
Learn what ya must learn
Do what ya can do

And tomorrow your nation
Will be what ya want it to be

Useni Eugene Perkins

AUGUST 8

There is no break

between

yesterday and today

mother and son

air and earth

all are a part

of the other

like

with this typewriter

I am connected

with these words

and these words

with this paper

and this paper with you.

Norman Jordan

SNAIL

Little snail,
Dreaming you go.
Weather and rose
Is all you know.

Weather and rose
Is all you see,
Drinking
The dewdrop's
Mystery.

Langston Hughes

TOMMY

I put a seed into the ground
And said, "I'll watch it grow."
I watered it and cared for it
As well as I could know.

One day I walked in my back yard,
And oh, what did I see!
My seed had popped itself right out,
Without consulting me.

Gwendolyn Brooks

81

KICK AND LIVE

Two ugly gray toads were hopping about,
   In the smooth, dewy grass soft as silk,
And they hopped to a cellar and fell through a hole
   Right into a great churn of milk.

"Now," said the first toad, "we're done for I'm sure
   And I know it is no use to try,
So I'll just give it up and sink in the milk,
   And go to the bottom and die."

So saying he sank deep down in the milk,
   And bubbles came up as he cried,
He struggled a while like a toad of his ilk,
   And then gave it all up and died.

Said toad number two, "I surely will try."
   And swiftly he commenced to kick.
"While I can keep from it, I'm not going to die,
   For I'm certain that I am not sick."

So he kicked till his limbs grew tired
　　And his little heart got in a flutter;
But he kept kicking on, determined to live,
　　Till he churned up a large cake of butter.

He then crawled on the butter to rest,
　　And get back his strength which was gone,
Took a good drink of milk and gave a great spring,
　　And landed safe out on the ground.

And now, stupid ones, take a lesson I pray,
　　From the brave little toad number two,
And just keep a-kicking and kicking away,
　　And make up your minds to get through.

If you fall into trouble which you can't understand,
　　Don't give up too quick with a sigh,
And go whirling down through the mire and the sand,
　　And sink to the bottom and die.

Just get up and kick and kick up and get,
　　Till you make a firm place on the ground,
Kick all of your troubles up into one set,
　　And then get upon them and bound.

G. W. Porter

83

TO CATCH A FISH

Dana went to catch a fish
He took his fishing pole
And cast his line into the lake
A chocolate cookie was his bait
He sat upon a rock to wait
To catch a great big fish

Suddenly he heard Blub Blub
Two fish stuck out their heads
"Offer us our favorite dishes
Worms or flies or smaller fishes
Maybe then you'll get your wish"
And off they swam, Blub Blub!

Nanette Mellage

84

I LOVE THE SEA

I love the sea! the rippling sea,
The ebbing, smiling, sunlit sea,
Hiding a world of mystery,
   Like you and me!

I love the sea! the placid sea,
The sleeping, glassy, silent sea,
Dreaming on long Eternity,
   Like you and me!

I love the sea! the heaving sea,
The mighty, moontost, angry sea,
Fretting from bondage to be free
   Like you and me!

Alfred M. Cruikshank

85

MOCKING BIRD

Miss Mocking Bird
is always heard
from high above the ground
For when you hear
a medley there
Miss Mocking Bird's around

Now we might find
birds of this kind
perched high atop a spire
Or we may see
one in a tree
or someplace even higher

Miss Mocking Bird
sings songs she's heard
from other birds nearby
She imitates
their sounds and makes
the people smile and sigh

For all day long
she'll sing her song
and whistle like a lark
Or she will coo
as pigeons do
when feeding in the park

And pretty soon
she'll change her tune
to something just as darling
Perhaps instead
she'll tilt her head
and croon just like a starling

Miss Gray Mocker
is a stocker
of bird songs great or small
With lots to know
she's never slow
to learn another call

So if you hear
Miss Mocker near
whistle your sweetest tune
And if you sing
a pretty thing
she may start mocking you

Nanette Mellage

ALL I AM

I'm a Blackbird
with golden wings
I'm a humming bird
who knows how to sing
I'm a silver shark
at the bottom
of the sea
I'm a rainbow fish
swimming comfortably
I'm a brown stallion
running across the field
I'm one of God's creations
who feels for real

Abiodun Oyewole

TO THE ZOO

I'm going to the zoo
    with you
        with you.
I'll try to stalk a lion
    and ride a kangaroo.

Then I'll climb a tall giraffe
    and laugh.
And laugh and laugh
    and LAUGH!

When I've had enough of zoo
I'll leave it and go home
    with you
        with you
            with you.

Lee Bennett Hopkins

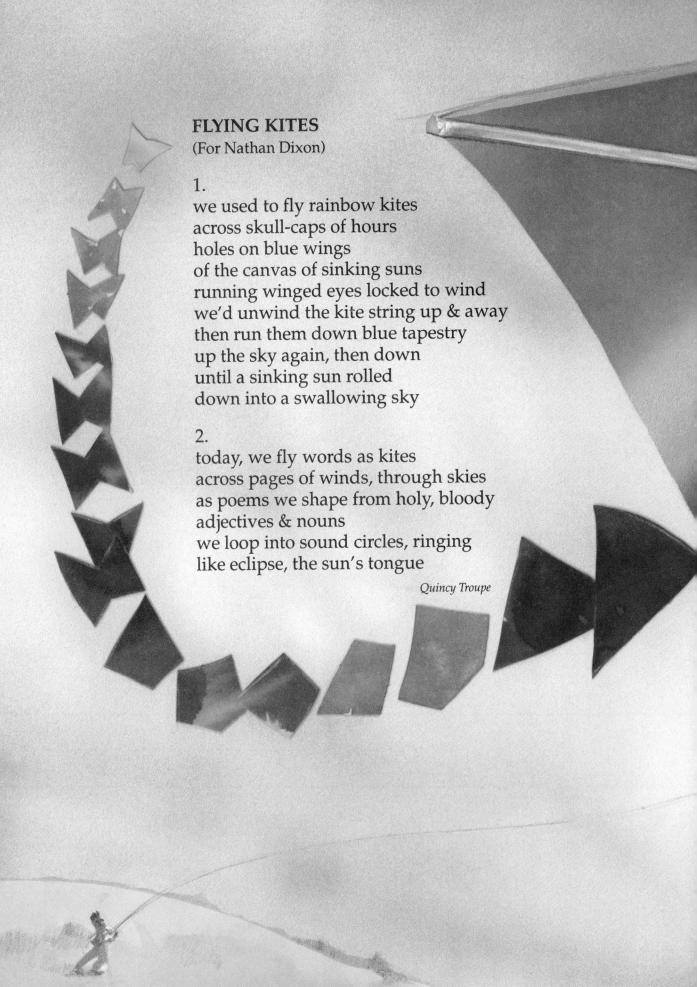

FLYING KITES
(For Nathan Dixon)

1.
we used to fly rainbow kites
across skull-caps of hours
holes on blue wings
of the canvas of sinking suns
running winged eyes locked to wind
we'd unwind the kite string up & away
then run them down blue tapestry
up the sky again, then down
until a sinking sun rolled
down into a swallowing sky

2.
today, we fly words as kites
across pages of winds, through skies
as poems we shape from holy, bloody
adjectives & nouns
we loop into sound circles, ringing
like eclipse, the sun's tongue

Quincy Troupe

90

THE POET SPEAKS

I know there seems to be
Little reason or rhyme
For poets who write of beauty
In such conflicting times . . .
But I am one of those
Who strive to yield,
Golden fruits, from stone fields.

John Henrik Clarke

BUTTERFLY

I had to leave the winter of my life
to find a summer place
to ease my heart of pain and strife
and leave this mad rat race
I had to fly away and take a chance
where trees are tall and green
where birds and flowers love to dance
and reality's a dream

    Butterfly am I
    velvet blue the sky
    yellow are my wings
    how I love to sing

    Butterfly am I
    velvet blue the sky
    yellow are my wings
    how I love to sing

I'd sing the song of sea and sand
and sail all through the hills
not certain of my destiny
just looking for my thrills
to laugh and play for just awhile
means so much to me
I feel much better when I smile
I feel like I am free

    Butterfly am I
    velvet blue the sky
    yellow are my wings
    how I love to sing

    Butterfly am I
    velvet blue the sky
    yellow are my wings
    how I love to sing

Abiodun Oyewole

MOVING RIGHT ALONG

Moving right along
finding my own way
as long as I sing my song
I'll reach the top one day
the road is long and wide
and there ain't no place to hide
from what you believe in yourself
to be true
so I must do what I got to do
and sing the song that suits my blues
so I've got to fly where I can glide
right through the magic of my life
and all of the walls that surround me
all of the falls that I take
I know that love is around me
and I will never break

Abiodun Oyewole

YOUR WORLD

Your world is as big as you make it.
I know, for I used to abide
In the narrowest nest in a corner,
My wings pressing close to my side.

But I sighted the distant horizon
Where the sky line encircled the sea
And I throbbed with a burning desire
To travel this immensity.

I battered the cordons around me
And cradled my wings on the breeze
Then soared to the uttermost reaches
With rapture, with power, with ease!

Georgia Douglas Johnson

IF SOMETIMES BLUE

It's a hard time situation
set up to make you blue.
Sometimes, it's a hard time situation
set up to make you blue.
That's why Mama said she
baked up sweet cakes and
told Dad to come home
with good news.

She said remember your good thing can
go bad sometimes
but
nothing goes bad always.
Remember, your good thing
can go bad sometimes, she said,
but
nothing goes bad always.
If a hard time situation gets
heavy chew on Mama's baked
memories recalling Dad's good news.

I said, people, sometimes
it's a hard time situation
set up to make you blue.
Sometimes it's a hard time situation
set up to make you blue.
That's why Mama said she
baked us sweet cakes and
told Dad to come home
each and every day with
some good news . . .
even if he had to fake it.

Alfred L. Woods

FIREFLIES

fireflies on night canvas
pulsating like glowing cat eyes
climbing now from hidden places
making their way to secret spaces
they swim through the darkness
speaking a silent language
of their mute lives, torn from roots
in flux & of their blinking light
forming the core of their movement
transparent, they are blown around
every notion of wind shift
flickering through ethereal darkness, where silence can be light:
wisdom searching for open doors

Quincy Troupe

ANOTHER MOUNTAIN

Sometimes there's a mountain
that I must climb
even after I've climbed one already
But my legs are tired now
and my arms need a rest
my mind is too weary right now
But I must climb before the storm comes
before the earth rocks
and an avalanche of clouds buries me
and smothers my soul
And so I prepare myself for another climb
Another Mountain
and I tell myself it is nothing
it is just some more dirt and stone
and every now and then I should reach
another plateau and enjoy the view
of the trees and the flowers below
And I am young enough to climb
and strong enough to make it to any top
You see the wind has warned me
about settling too long
about peace without struggle
The wind has warned me
and taught me how to fly
But my wings only work
After I've climbed a mountain

Abiodun Oyewole

WINTER POEM

once a snowflake fell
on my brow and i loved
it so much and i kissed
it and it was happy and called its cousins
and brothers and a web
of snow engulfed me then
i reached to love them all
and i squeezed them and they became
a spring rain and i stood perfectly
still and was a flower

Nikki Giovanni

SCIENCE . . .

Science
   tells you
      Black is the
         absence of light

but
   your soul
      tells you Black
         is the light of the
           world.

Gordon Nelson

DREAMS

Hold fast to dreams
For if dreams die
Life is a broken-winged bird
That cannot fly.

Hold fast to dreams
For when dreams go
Life is a barren field
Frozen with snow.

Langston Hughes

THE DREAM KEEPER

Bring me all of your dreams,
You dreamer,
Bring me all our your
Heart melodies
That I may wrap them
In a blue cloud-cloth
Away from the too-rough fingers
Of the world.

Langston Hughes

Index of Titles

Index of First Lines

Index of Poets

About the Poets

WILLIAM STANLEY BRAITHWAITE (1878-1962) was born in Boston, Massachusetts, in 1878 to West Indian parents. Self-educated, he developed a love for literature while apprenticed to a printer. In addition to writing poetry, he edited several poetry anthologies. *The Annual Anthology of Magazine Verse*, which he edited between 1913 and 1929, presented poems by several unknown writers who later became famous. His own work was greatly influenced by English romantic poets and is noted for its artistic delicacy and its lack of racial themes.

GWENDOLYN BROOKS (1917-   ) was born in Topeka, Kansas, but lived in Chicago, Illinois, from the age of one month. She has written many books of poetry and has edited poetry anthologies. Her poetry has earned her many honors, including, in 1950, the first Pulitzer Prize ever awarded to a black writer. She has taught at several universities, and received many honorary doctorates. She is the Poet Laureate of Illinois. Her poetry is influenced by English romantic poetry, but she writes about being black and a woman in contemporary America.

JOHN HENRIK CLARKE (1915-   ) was born in Union Springs, Alabama. He studied at New York University, Columbia University, and the New School for Social Research. He is Professor Emeritus of African and World History at Hunter College. Clarke has edited twenty-six books, including *Harlem U.S.A.* and several biographies of prominent African-Americans.

LUCILLE CLIFTON (1936-   ) was born in Depew, New York. She attended Howard University, then Fredonia State Teachers College. She is known for her poetry about life in the ghetto and about family relationships. The poet has served as a writer-in-residence at Columbia University and George Washington University and has taught literature and creative writing at the University of California at Santa Cruz.

ALFRED M. CRUIKSHANK lived in the West Indies. He wrote poetry to describe his feelings, the people he knew, and the neighborhood he lived in and loved.

COUNTEE CULLEN (1903-1946) was born in New York City. After the death of his grandmother, he was brought up by the Reverend Frederick A. Cullen, the pastor of Harlem's largest congregation, a leading figure in the cultural and political life of Black America at that time. Countee received recognition for his poetry while attending New York City's public schools and continued to win praise for his writing as a student at New York University and later at Harvard. His first book of poems, published upon graduation from college, established him as a force in the Harlem Renaissance. He believed that art and poetry could rise above the question of race, although many of his poems do address this issue. His poetry uses wit to comment on the human condition. He spent several years teaching English, and he has written books of poetry for children.

MARI EVANS, educator, writer, musician, resides in Indianapolis. Formerly Distinguished Writer and Assistant Professor, ASRC, Cornell University, she has taught at universities around the country. She is the author of numerous articles, four children's books, several performed theater pieces, two musicals, and four volumes of poetry. She edited the highly acclaimed *Black Women Writers (1950-1980): A Critical Evaluation*.

KARAMA FUFUKA (1951-) was born in Chicago, Illinois, and she attended the University of Illinois and Loop City College. She enjoys writing poetry and stories for children. She has often worked with her husband, who is a writer and illustrator of children's books.

NIKKI GIOVANNI (1943-   ) was born in Knoxville, Tennessee, but moved to Cincinatti, Ohio, while still a child. Her memories of growing up in these places provide her with subject matter for much of her poetry for children. She is known worldwide for the many books of poetry that she has written for children and adults. Her work has appeared in numerous publications and has been read on television. She has taught college students and traveled around the United States reciting her poems. Her poetry, sometimes about black consciousness and sometimes about the search for self, is always about love.

ELOISE GREENFIELD has written many prize-winning books for children. Her poems and stories are often about black heritage, especially the African-American experience, and they are written in a way that makes young people think about themselves and their world. She shares her love of writing by teaching creative writing to schoolchildren in Washington, D.C.

KALI GROSVENOR (1960-   ), whose mother is also an author, began to write poems when she was just six years old. Her first book of poems was published when she was just eight. She lives and works in Washington, D.C.

LEE BENNETT HOPKINS grew up in Newark, New Jersey. He attended Kean College and the Bank Street College of Education and later earned a diploma in Educational Supervision and Administration from Hunter College. He taught elementary school for several years and served as a consultant to school systems around the United States and Canada, to a television series for children, and to other educational organizations. He is the author of three novels and several professional books and articles. He is the editor of more than thirty poetry anthologies.

DAKARI KAMAU HRU is a poet and a storyteller. He has taught poetry and writing to children all over New York City, where he lives, and has appeared on national television as part of the International Black Storytelling Festival.

LANGSTON HUGHES (1902-1967), born in Joplin, Missouri, is one of the great poets of the Harlem Renaissance. He received recognition for his writing while still in high school, where he was elected Class Poet in his senior year. After graduation he lived for a year with his father in Mexico City before attending Columbia University. However, he dropped out after one year and supported himself with various jobs in New York and Europe. He returned to the United States and was working in a Washington, D.C. hotel when his poetry attracted the attention of other poets and the press. In 1926 his first collection, *Weary Blues,* was published. He then returned to school, graduating from Lincoln University in Pennsylvania. In addition to poetry, Hughes wrote novels, newspaper articles, songs, historical works, and books for children. His poetry is not bound by traditional poetic forms or subjects. He often incorporated folk and jazz rhythms in his work and wrote about life as he saw it.

GEORGIA DOUGLAS JOHNSON (1880-1966), born in Atlanta, Georgia, attended Atlanta University and the Oberlin Conservatory of Music. Although she considered becoming a composer, she took a job as a high school teacher and then held various government posts in Washington, D.C. She was a prolific writer. In addition to four books of poetry, she wrote plays, songs, and fiction and has worked as a journalist. Her Washington home was an important meeting place for writers and artists.

NORMAN JORDAN (1938-   ) was born in Ansted, West Virginia. His formal education was interrupted early when he dropped out of Junior High School and began to work, first as a laborer and then as a highway inspector. Later, he went on to work with young people at a youth center in Cleveland, Ohio. He has written books of poetry, and his poems have been published in anthologies. He has also written plays, several of which have been produced.

DOUGHTRY LONG (1942-   ) was born in Atlanta, Georgia. He has written several books of poetry, and his work has been published in many anthologies.

BARBARA MAHONE (1944-   ) was born in Chicago, Illinois. Her poems have been published in several anthologies. Her first collection of poetry, *Sugarfields*, apeared in 1970.

CEDRIC MCCLESTER (1946-) was born in Boston, Massachusetts. He attended the College for Human Services and Fordham University, earning a B.A. in Professional Studies —Human Services and an M.S. in Education. He is a member of the New York Association of Black Journalists. He has written for national and international publications. Formerly a syndicated columnist, his columns appeared in the largest black weeklies in New York and New Jersey, *Big Red* and *New Jersey Connection*. He is the author of *Kwanza: Everything You Always Wanted to Know but Didn't Know Where to Ask*.

NANETTE MELLAGE, an actress, poet, and storyteller, lives and works in New England. She has worked in children's and adult theater, and enioys retelling folktales from all over the world.

GORDON NELSON (1953-   ) was born in Bronx, New York. He is a poet and playwright whose musical, *The Legacy: Memories of Gospel Song*, played at the National Black Theater for three years. He now lives in Mount Vernon, New York.

ABIODUN OYEWOLE began writing poetry as a boy — and has never stopped. In 1968, in an atmosphere of political and social activism, he formed a group called "The Last Poets" who tried to reach out and educate people through poetry. In addition to poems, Oyewole writes plays which have been performed in many communities around the United States. He is also the leading member of a jazz group called Griot (gree-o) which means "African storyteller." He is committed to young people and has written many poems for children.

USENI EUGENE PERKINS lives and works in Chicago, Illinois. He is a poet, a playwright, and a sociologist who has devoted his life to writing for and about children. He has published several books of social commentary about African-American youth and is considered to be an expert in this area. He is the editor of the *Black Child Journal*.

SONIA SANCHEZ (1935-   ) was born in Birmingham, Alabama. Her poems explore the themes of black heritage and black identity and often incorporate rhythms and language from urban America. The poet emphasizes the performance of her work, linking it to the African oral tradition. She has read her poems around the world and on more than five hundred college campuses.

QUINCY TROUPE was born and raised in St. Louis, Missouri, and is the son of the second greatest catcher in the history of the all-black baseball leagues. He is professor of American and Third World Literature at the College of Staten Island and teaches writing to graduate students at Columbia University. He has taught at colleges in California, Ohio, Ghana, and Nigeria. In addition to three books of poetry, he has published books about the arts, works of fiction, and many essays and articles. He is the editor of a number of literary journals. Troupe currently lives and works in New York City.

ALFRED L. WOODS was born in Pell City, Alabama. He attended the University of Illinois at Chicago and Champaign-Urbana, where he received a Masters of Library Science. Woods has been writing since high school. His work has appeared in numerous publications, and collections of his poetry have been published. He served as the Executive Director of both the Illinois Library Association and the South Side Community Art Center in Chicago.

We have tried to include a biographical note about each poet whose work appears in this book, but we have not been successful in some instances. We would be grateful for any further information that could be included in future editions.

It is fitting that the first book published by Checkerboard
Press, Inc., a newly independent publishing house, should be
Make a Joyful Sound, a book that carries a message of hope and joy.
We believe that what we do really does matter, and that when it
matters to all of us, then we can truly make a difference.

We begin with the hope that children everywhere will be
entertained, encouraged, and enlightened by the poems in this
book. So here's hoping that we do, in fact, make a joyful sound.

Terry Savoy
President
New York, 1991

The illustrators, **CORNELIUS VAN WRIGHT AND YING-HWA HU,**
are a husband and wife artist team living in New York City. Cornelius
was born in New York and studied art at the School of Art and Design
and the School of Visual Arts. Ying-Hwa was born in Taipei, Taiwan.
She studied at Shi Chen College and at St. Cloud State University.
She is a former art teacher. The two artists have illustrated
many books for children.

The artists created the illustrations for this book on Bristol board, using
color and graphite pencils,watercolors, and dyes applied with brush
and airbrush.

The text of this book was set in Palatino typeface.

The book was designed by Tom Koken.